Sweet White Wine
And
Red Biddy Rambling

More than two years of Lockdown, when, as a vulnerable person and one of the Prime Carers for one of an even more vulnerable age, the isolation caused a creative spurt.

This, coupled with the leadership of a Prime Minister twice sacked for lying and widely regarded as a congenital liar, and a Government allegedly corrupt, found guilty of misleading our Queen, and under police investigation for breaking their own laws, made of it a fascinating period.

Here's the result. Two years of an active mind working in a trapped body. The relief when partial, release came, was tangible.

The result, I hope,is interesting.

Contents

AD 2022
Sweet White Wine
IntellSpeak
The Coal man Cometh
Prime Numbers
Cold War Country Rock
HouseOf Cats
By Design
Subservience
Bartered Britain
On Social Media
Missing
By Appointment
Our Mighty River
Precision Swearing
Seven Years Between
Mother Of Parliaments
Post Big Bang
Veggie
Dr Spooner Rules,Ok?
My Way
Snippet ii
Performing Poets
Whispers Of Eternity
Conspiracy Theory
Trolley Dolly
The Needle's Eye
Whipped in
When I'm 65
Passings
Why
Love Poem For A Rainy Day
Respect
Learning From History
Sleep

Contingency Planning
Music Revolutionaries
Red Biddy Rambling
Sandman
Jingles
Everlasting life
Self Destruction
Black And White
Natural Selection
Old Friend
On Continuous Creation
Human Relations
White Rum And Coke
Trauma Part i
Trauma Part ii
Street Walker
Wealth
Slipping Away
The Fish Stealer
For Services Rendered
Modern Day Warrior

AD 2022

May the few learn to conquer
Their avarice and greed
So that none may live
In poverty and need
May we learn humanity
May we learn to share
So that none may die
Denied basic health care.
May those of religion learn to read
What their scriptures teach
May they walk in peace
And practice what they preach
May we start to heal the world
Remove ignorance and fear
May the world start to progress
So this be a truly Happy New Years
Amen, amen, amen

Sweet White Wine

We smooched around the floor
Her body pressed tight to mine
I was high on stout and scotch
She on gin and sweet white wine
And we swayed around that room
In a world all of our very own
Engrossed each with the other
Part of a crowd but really all alone
In that room of spinning lights
And smoke and heat and noise
In that room of search and seek
Of single girls and single boys
Each body peeled from the other
As the music came briefly to an end
And in that intermission
Each found another friend
And the smooching re started
The dancing cheek to cheek
Friday night relaxation
After a long long week
Just as the last waltz started
She slid back into my embrace
Body moulded back to body
Pleasure painted on her face
And we knew how we knew
How our evening would end
For things just can't be any better
When you lover is your best friend
We smooched around the floor
Her body pressed tight to mine
I was high on stout and scotch
She on gin and sweet white wine

IntellSpeak

We used to listen to the Radio
Five minutes News on the hour
Middle of the road voices
Not too light or too dour.
Now we have twenty four hour TV
With accompanying twenty four news
And a specialist breed of expert on call
To discuss, give opinions and air views.
I think they come from distant lands
With an exotic language they speak,
Suited for every single situation
No matter how apparently bleak.
It's full of special phrases,
Full of jargon too,
And they'll never use one word
If there's a chance of using two.
I think they're hired for the intellectual,
Not a working class peasant like me,
Minimum intellectual standard seems
An upper second Oxbridge degree.
They all seem to know each other,
Seem to come in groups of four,
And unless they're controlled
All can talk for evermore.
I'm sure they could spout
All the day long
Secure in the certitude
They're never ever wrong.
Please, could we have some experts
The common herd can understand,
Not these self certified speakers
From their Intellectually elitist land.
And, it would be more than helpful if,
For even just one day each week,
They would pay heed to the general

And use a language we all speak.
But, there's a special terminology
All those experts use
When they're waxing forth eloquent
On TwentyFour Hour TV News.

The Coal Man Cometh

About the end of times when
Carts were hauled by Shires,
Coal was king and homes
Were heated by open fires,
A seemingly huge dark figure
From my early childhood days
As he drove his horse and cart
Through the country byways
From village to village to village
Delivering sacks of coal
To feed our coal fires, then
Each home's heart and soul.

One hundredweight of coal
Measured into each heavy sack
Which they'd hoist off the cart
Onto a waiting broad back
To be carried to the coal shed
To be skilfully slipped
And with ease of movement
Very carefully tipped
Not a black lump wasted
As it piled on the coal heap
For money was tight
And coal wasn't cheap.

His horse patiently standing
By each house's kerb side
Waiting to be led on or
For him to climb up and ride.
Hours they must have spent
Huddled on that cart seat
Muffled up for winter's cold
Or soaking up summer's heat.
One day suddenly, progress,

The Shire retired out to grass
The second hand liveried lorry
Shelter behind steel and glass.

Still a hard dirty job but warmer
As the world moved slowly on
King Coal was coldly murdered
And the job was virtually gone.
Just a figure from history
From a simpler, slower age
Not even meriting a foot note
On a social history primer's page.
Is there a niche in time and space
Where a coal man and his horse,
Waggon piled with sacks, eternally
Trundles his once essential course

Prime Numbers

He found a Prime number that
Was so incredibly long
It took hours Just to check that
He hadn't transcribed it wrong.
His discovery had been result
Of such a painstaking search
The fruit of of many hours of
Dedicated, careful research.
He was only a young man
His career only just begun
Pale from lack of time spent
Outside there in the sun.
He looked up from his PC
To see a clear blue sky
Felt the heat on his face
And asked himself why.

The world of academia lost
A mathematician for awhile
As he decided it was time
He changed his life style.
He walked the National Parks
A tent upon his back
Spent many hours wandering
Way off the beaten track.
Feeling rejuvenated
He organised his working day
Into three separate sections
Of rest, work and play
Too much labour
And not enough joy
Could make a person into
A dull and dreary boy.

His search for Prime Numbers

Continued with success
Even though he'd decided
To work a lot of hours less
And because he wasn't tired
It didn't take him so long
With a vastly reduced chance
Of transcribing any of them wrong.
They may think it's esoteric
Study in such an obscure field
But all that time and effort can
Bring many a great security yield,
For use of the Prime Number
Can take any message spoken
And encrypt it in a code
Very unlikely to be broken

Cold War Country Rock

Four o'clock in the morning,
Another four hours to go,
Mouth tastes of stomach acid
Eyes like pee holes in the snow.
Every Mid shift at this time
It's always the same
Time to start playing
My stay awake game.
Me and old Elvis playing music
On our imaginary record show,
Country Rock mainly
For those in the know.

A quick check around
For duty's sake
Just to make sure
Everybody's still awake.
Pete on station four
Is starting to nod.
The Op next door
Gives him a sly prod.
Back to the music.
Wish I could close my eyes,
But that's just when sleep
Catches you by surprise.

Cold War Berlin, Cuban Crisis
Still in full swing,
Nobody quite knowing
What problems it will bring.
Whatever they may be
We're all hoping they'll keep,
Just another four hours
Then it's off to bed to sleep.
Elvis racks the records

With the coming of full light.
Together we've survived
Yet another sleepless night.

Four more days
That will just fly away
And we're off again
It's another Mid Shift Day
Start off bright and cheerful
But it just isn't right
To be awake and sober
In the middle of the night.
Old Elvis is waiting
For me to say okay
The deck is off and spinning
Our programme's under way.

House Of Cats

This was once a house of Catts
Sometimes two, three, even four,
A house once ruled by the not
Always so gentle little gentle paw.
That little poke in
The middle of the night,
Just to check
You're still alright,
And you might as well,
Now you're awake
Serve a little food
For pity's sake.
I said food.
I'm not eating that
Do you think I'm one
Of those common cats.
I know some times it
Sounds absurd
But I've been reduced
To eating a bird
Even at times
A humble mouse
I left one somewhere.
Around the house.
Stop being awkward
Can't you just see.
It's that right time
That I sit on your knee.
I'm a creature of beauty
Character and charm,
Sleeping peacefully
Over your unused arm.
Now I'm going outside.
I don't quite know when
But I'll be back

When you're needed again.
Yes this used to be a house of cats,:
A house of purring , miaowing hissing
No cats are living here now:
Sadly, I think, there's something missing.

By Design

For centuries things developed
All on their own
The thinking being if it worked
Just leave it alone,
Then along came the Designer
With their very different creed
Of interfering with our things
Even when there was no need.

The very attractive implement
Now no longer fit for use
Having been subject of
A Re-design abuse.
Those impractical artefacts
That look so very nice
Thanks to the Designer Label
Now costing three times the price.

Before I die just grant me
A baseball bat and one hour alone
With that accursed designer of
The Automated Answerphone.
Is it being too selfish to ask chance
To give them a thorough pasting
For all the hours they caused
Me to spend fruitlessly wasting.

Grant one hour withThe inventor
of the canned music machine
I'd make the thoughtless wretch wish
His existence had never been.
If it ain't broke don't fix it
Should be imprinted in every brain
So at least there's a chance these
Creatures will stop driving us insane.

There are people in this world who
Strive to make our lives finer.
Sadly that doesn't apply to most of.
That idiot class called Designer.
Is it too much to ask to be
Granted my philanthropic need
To rid the world of at least one of
That odious thoughtless breed.

Subservience

I'm a member of the working class
Thankful just to be alive
Grateful the sweat of my brow helps
My betters to survive.
I pay me taxes willingly
I don't have any cares
That my betters routinely
Evade and avoid paying theirs
I serve my social betters
Do all that they could ask
Faithfully and reliably carry out
Their every appointed task.
Eat the crumbs from their table,
Show them all due respect
Receive the odd recognition
Which is all I can expect.
I live a meagre existence
Struggle from day to day
Show my gratitude for my
Below subsistence rate of pay.
I wave my Union Flag,
Sing God Save Our Queen
And when I slip quietly into death
It'll be as though I've never been.

Bartered Britannia

Bartered Britannia
Dodgiest of States
Ruled by coterie
Of dodgy mates.
Treaties signed
To be broken,
Pledges ignored
As soon as spoken.
Offshore island,
Once of esteem,
Now existing
On past dreams.
Placid inhabitants
Desensitised,
Or, perhaps,
Lobotomised
When it comes
To the election game
Mindlessly vote for
More of the same.

On Social Media

You blew me a kiss
Across the internet
But in real life
We never met.
We chatted happily
Nearly every day
Each finding enough
Things to say.
The internet being such
A peculiar place,
Only fantasy meetings
Never face to face

So, as the days passed
As, by and by
Found nothing in common
You and I,
Realising soon that
If we ever did meet
We'd avoid each other
By crossing the street.
Just an acquaintance,
Not a friend,
Time I think for
Our converse to end.

So it's goodbye,
Thanks for the the chat,
But I think we've both
Had enough on that.
I wish you joy
In all you do.
Please, don't call me,
And I won't call you.
I've learned my lesson,

Chosen to succeed yeah
With hours long sessions
On good old Wikipedia.

Missing

As he was walking down the street
One foot fell off,
An embarrassing incident
He manage to cover with a cough.
Just twenty yards further
To his despair
He discovered that
He wasn't even there.
Time, he thought, to
End his roam
So he turned about and
Walked back home
There he realised,
With a wince,,
He wasn't in.
Nobody's seen him since.
There's just a space
Where he used to be
And cup of cold
Unsweetened tea
And the impression
Of one foot
In a pile
Of fallen soot.
So ends
This sad sad tale of sorrow
Gone today
And still gone tomorrow.
Just occasionally someone
May almost meet
A one footed man
Not quite there on the street.

By Appointment

The Westminster Palace dealer
And the service he affords
Is precise and efficient whether
For the Commons or the Lords.
He arrives for every sitting
In his classic Mini Moke
Using calibrated scales
For his top grade coke
Which he never ever cuts
Just precisely weighs
And carefully seals in
Recyclable paper sachets.
His service may be illegal
But he likes it to be seen
As far as humanly possible
It's one hundred percent green.
The Westminster Palace dealer
A service of courtesy and style
The Westminster Palace dealer
Top class produce with a smile.

Our Mighty River

Now spanned by her bridge
Gracefully curving the air,
A politicians' prank once
Dubbed Road to Nowhere,
She's an estuarial river,
Fast and very wide
That can threaten the City
With her Spring Tide
Or, when onshore storm wind
Holds tidal waters back,
Breach barriers that can't always
Withstand such attack.
Most times it's fine but
Sometimes it's close and able
To top them and cause flood
Helped by our high water table.

We are a maritime City
Built on reclaimed flood plains
Used to high waters through
Outdated overloaded drains.
Majestic on a summers day
A real sight to be seen
Flowing fast to the North Sea
A burnished wide silver sheen.
A confluence of rivers flowing
From the moors wolds and dales
A spectacular sight when
She's whipped along by the gales.
She's treacherous and dangerous
And many a Master's given thanks
For skilled Humber Pilot's steerage
Through shifting channels and banks.

Our River Humber once taking fleets,
Whaling, trawling, deep sea trade,
Building up the hardy character
Of which our citizens are made.
We are a city built on water
For better or worse, bad or good
The steady flowing of our river is like
A heart pumping out our city's life blood
A City that at times has
Seen its ambitions shattered
Beaten down but never beaten
A historic city, bombed, battered,
Entering the twenty first century as if
Newly wakened from its long slumber
Split by the tidal river Hull, standing
On the banks of the mighty Humber.

Precision Swearing

Precision swearing they call it
A term that may sound absurd
But it's economical with the breath
And wastes not a single word,
It rolls smoothly from the tongue
Instantly relieving pain
And, in the case of mental turmoil
Relieves stress and strain.
Better for use in private
When one can really let rip,
Out in public One feels
one should really keep a grip.
No perverted back street cursing.
No random state of mind
No ranting and raving
Of the common peasant kind
A selection of eloquent phrases.
Not all of them in general use
All carefully, precisely chosen
To avoid any language abuse.
An unappreciated form of therapy
That is readily there to explore
A bout of precision cursing
Satisfying to the very core.
Throw away your tranquillisers
Throw away your happy pills
A bout of precision swearing can
Remedy so many common ills.

Seven Years Betwwen

When were rutted tracks replaced
By smoothly metalled roads
And petrol engined lorries replaced
Horse drawn waggon loads?
My brother was born
In that period in between
With a parity of horses and
Petrol driven machine.
Just seven years older
But five of them were war
And it was a different world
From that gone on before.
And the advent of peace
So changed the situation
That he and I might have been
Separated by generations

He the labouring rustic
Working hard on the farm
Me the Grammar school boy
No need for the strong arm.
Two very different lives
But right to the very end
He remained not just a brother
But an old and valued friend.
So many times we chatted
About the changes there had been
Caused by that bloody war and
Those seven years in between
I think of him in the village
Every time I go back
And wander down a remaining
Unmetalled rutted cart track.

Mother Of Parliaments

The Mother of Parliament
Is that coming to an end,
Manned by pimps and whores
Ever ready to help a friend?
They bend and change its rules
Openly more and more
Act in the House as though
They are all above the law.

They don't even bother
To use guile or stealth
As they steadily acquire more
And more of the Nation's wealth.
How long must we endure
Their contemptuous misrule
How long will we remain
This Nation of spineless fools

Stand to attention
As they fly the Union Jack
For what it's worth, in theory,
We've all got our country back!
Once the Mother of Parliaments
A state they pretend to still
As the pimps and the whores
Daily dip their fingers in the till.

Post Big Bang

The James Webb Telescope
Has arrived in position at last
All ready to start looking back
Into the far distant past
Possibly in due course
Achieving the situation
Where they are seeing that
Very instant after creation
imagine what could be
Their state of surprise
If at the other end they saw
A pair of watching back eyes.
And hanging there in space
A large optical device
Devised and installed by
An eternal version of Karl Zeiss

Veggie

To all my Veggie mates
Can I ask you a favour?
Why does so much
Of your food
Seem to have
Fake animal flavour?,
No intention
To offend.
Just asking
For a friend.

Dr Spooner's Rules, OK?

His affliction caused him distress
At times, I understand
But, thank you Dr Spooner
For the gift you gave this land.
Innocuous little phrases
Cause pleasure and surprise
When they're first heard
After being Spoonerised.
That watched pot
That never boils
Now the patched wot
That bever noils

The quality of mercy
That's never strained
The mality of quercy
That's strever nained.
The common phrase
Song of a bird
Achieves mystery as
The bong of a sird.
I get great joy from
This form of wordplay
Which, in truth, I practise
Almost every single day.

You can almost feel
The frustration of predictive text
When it tries to forecast
What you'll be typing next.
Thanks again Dr Spooner
For your gonderful wift
Which has given many an hour
Such a londerful wift.
I'm sorry on occasion

It caused you dismay
For me it's transformed
Many a dundane may.

My Way

I string my words together
In my own simple way.
Some people say they like them
Some people say they're ok,
And I can stand on a stage and
Make an audience want to hear
And the pleasure never lessens
No matter how often I appear,

The musicians then follow
And between tunes they pause
And whatever their ability
They always receive applause.
I have no musical talent
I just can't play
Any instrument
In even a basic way.

I just cant compete with them
I just holler like a loon
Because I can't keep a rhythm
And I can't hold a tune
I'm my mind I'm a Sinatra but
the facts don't bear that out
And when it comes to harmony
I'm always the odd one out.

I wish i could sing like Johnny
And wish I could write like Kris
I wish I could play like Django
But I just keep on doing this.
I can see their interest
Reflected in their faces
And they always seem to listen
And laugh in the right places

I don't pretend to be an intellectual
I try to keep meter and use thyme
And if you don't understand
I just think I've wasted our time
just stringing my words together
In my own simple way
Some people say they like them
Some people say i do ok.

Snippet ii

He took a hesitant first step,
Then another two or three,
And then he was marching
Straight out into the sea
They found his body two days
Later, brought in by the tide
They'd no idea why
He'd taken that first stride.
No indication of problems
That made him seek release
Just on his face an expression
Of absolute calm and peace

Performing Poets

They stand there for ages
Pouring out angst and woe,
Seeming to gain strength
As their words start to flow.
They curse and they swear,
Stand, scream and shout,
And I've really no idea
What they're talking about.
Just these loud strident voices
Hammering away in my head
I'm losing the will to live
I've long lost the thread.
If you thrive on your misery
Then that's just fine
Done make me feel guilty for
A happy out look like mine.

I came here full of optimism
But now I'm near suicidal,
Reflecting on the merits of
The old Scolds Bridal,
A quick burst with a taser
Even E.C.T. shocks
Maybe even an hour or so
Chaining them up in the stocks.
I'm finished, I'm leaving
Driven out at last,
Just a relict from
Their very recent past.
I've always supped
From the half full cup.
Just a final message,
For God's sake, lighten up.

Whispers Of Eternity

You can hear the sound of creation
Quietly whispering through space
Last remnants of the explosion from
When The Big Bang first took place,
That in time formed the first stars,
Can still hear sound of that reaction
Starting off the expansion
That ended in contraction
And, so the process continued,
No indication of hurry or haste
And they say in this long process
Never an iota of any material waste.
Every atom of every element used
Over and over and over again
A constant recycling so that
Never any matter loss or gain.
Everything is made of stardust,
Even beings like you or I
And we return to stardust
When we eventually die.

And eons in the future
We may have drifted so far
To be part of the substances
That coalesce to birth a new star.
In the context of the universe
Is that not a type of rebirth,
Being part of a star that in time may
Nurture and harbour a new Earth.
A beautiful concept as the universe
Renews and steadily moves on
So that in one form or another
A being is never ever truly gone.
Maybe with no consciousness
Maybe without any soul

Maybe not even a sense of ,
Being the part of a new whole.
There are stars in nurseries
Just waiting to fully form m
Made from matter of the dead
In that celestial renewal norm.

Conspiracy Theory

It's just a huge conspiracy.
Facebook says it's so,
And, it's a well known fact,
The experts on Facebook know
The City seems so quiet now
Just a littered and dirty street
Now the anti vaxxers have gone,
Their demonstration complete.
Hardly the peaceful promised demo
For they stood, cursed and swore,
Issued threats and insults to folk
About the face coverings they wore.
And, as always, hidden in the centre
The balaclava'd active mob
Stirring up the others with
Their big and strident gobs.

The scientists from Facebook
Who absolutely know it all,
Those Rent-A-Mob Heroes
Always there on constant call.
If they sadly catch the virus I hope
After all they've ranted and raved
They'll stand by their convictions
And not expect their lives saved.
After all the law allowed them
To publicly raise their voice
And they were all allowed
To exercise their free choice,
And it is just a conspiracy
So I'd want to know just why
They don't stick to their convictions
And quietly just go off and die.

Trolley Dolly

Christopher Robin's thinking of Alice
But she wasn't with him there
Alice was above the Indian Ocean
Ten thousand feet up in the Air,
Working as a Trolley Dolly
First Class Section, Exotic Air Line,
Mixing with the Jet Set and
Finding life suited her just fine.

She'd joined the Mile High Club,
Just to give it a try
Wondering if making love was different
Performed way up in the sky.
So many beautiful people seen daily
In her normal working life,
Maybe the chance of becoming
A very rich man's wife.

Alice loved her occupation
Of which she was justly proud
Until one day her airliner
Just disappeared into a cloud.
Christopher Robin mourned his Alice
Thought of all those things he didn't say
Then he sadly closed his heart
And let life take him on its way.

The Needle's Eye

Just send us money monthly,
The TV campaigns plead,
For various worthy causes
Each with its specific need:
Clean drinking water,
Help rescue a cat
Refugees in need,
Causes as varied as that.
And, the wealth gap enlarges
Concentrated in less and less hands
As The ruling elite milk the resources
Of the many and varied lands.
So, the world just keeps on turning,
The dispossessed still starve and die
And nobody seems to think
To ask the question why
The charities keep on asking
The less wealthy for more and more
While, from their state of opulence,
The rich casually ignore
The worsening predicament
Of their fellow man
Because their situation
Just allows that they can.
Nightly the television
Entreats us all to give.
Just twenty pounds a month
Will allow stray dogs to live.
Perhaps in these modern times
That old adage doesn't apply
About the camel, the rich man,
Heaven, and the needle's eye.

Whipped In

He was a professor of difficult sums,
Thought in quadratic equations
And from the works of Lobachevsky
He could spew forth quotations.
But, he had a hidden secret,
Not a creature of the light,
Dressed in Robin Hood suit
He prowled through the night.
Many a homeward bound drunk
Had doubted what he'd seen,
This tall, bow bearing figure
Dressed in suit of Lincoln Green.
But, here's the little twist
To our hero's unusual story,
He robbed the poor to help the rich
Like many a card bearing Tory.
His nemesis came in the shape of
One Detective Constable Brown
Whose reactions to his demands
Was to quickly Taser him down.
He's a reformed character now for
They only gave a year's probation
And lots of Community Service
Teaching mathematics to the Nation.
And, so, as time quickly passes
That's the way that he becomes
Appointed to the House of Lords
As the Minister for Difficult Sums,
His Criminal Record now regarded
As just a small mental aberration.
He's feted, lauded and regarded
As a flower of this Great Nation.
He follows the whip zealously,
But deep down inside he plots
To maximise his expenses claims,
A leopard seldom changes its spots.
Thank heaven he's in the Lords or

It could have been more sinister:
We could have had a thief and liar
Serving as our new Prime Minister.

When I'm 65 ....

They still talk of it in Neasden
And all places North and South
Mainly on the internet or by
Whispered word of mouth
How they found him bleeding
With injuries to his face
First hit and run victim of
An illegal mobility scooter race
As they occupied the pavements
Converging on the town
Screaming out their warnings
Before mowing people down
There was crisis in the kingdom
As the mass movement grew
For by magic of the internet
All the silver surfers knew
Their progress was urgent
For while they were at large
Demands had to be met before
Scooters ran out of charge
The authorities vacillated
Reeling under the assault
Until in a deathly silence
The convoys came to silent halt
Not meant to be continuously driven
For much more than an hour
The liberating chariots suddenly
Ran completely out of power
The powers that be now rejected
Their very reasonable demands
Of free scooter parking with
All free recharging stands
Ringleaders were sectioned
And their scooters confiscated
And all too very soon

The rebellion had abated
An uneasy peace
Lay across the land
As the authorities disbursed
That bold rebellious band
But sometimes in the night
Their story still gets told
Of the day they fought for rights
For the disabled and the old
And the authorities made concessions
Never quite knowing when
The spirit of freedom being rekindled
The pensioners would rebel again

Passings

Random Meeting and partings
Very pleasant conversations
Spread over some years between
Men of very different generations
First occurrence at The Blues Bar
Long London weekend away
Pleasantly chatting as we both
Listened to the birthday boy play.

Musicians wedding day in Saltaire
Some few years having moved on
Renewing a pleasant acquaintance
Speculating on those years gone
This year meeting at the funeral
A beloved Matriarch's passing
Just a few short words spoken
At the wake just mainly in passing.

Pleasant conversations over years
This time just a little speculation
Wondering when we'd meet again
And what would be the occasion
Some people make a difference
Just by their being there
Some people make that effort
Just to show respect and care.

Why

Don't call me a Hero.
You weren't even there
When I got the wound
That put me in this chair.
I was doing my duty
Patrolling disputed ground
It was just random chance
That I took a sniper's round.

You didn't see me
Moaning and crying
Totally convince I was
Bleeding out and dying.
No, the Hero was my mate
Who applied dressings that day
And stayed there with me until
The medics could take me away.

Heroes don't wake up screaming
In the middle of the night
Because the bloody flashbacks
Have them convulsed with fright.
It would be wonderful, if,
Just for one special day,
I was there as myself,
Not as the Hero on display.

Please don't call me a Hero
It's such a status to live up to
And when I let you down
As I so often do
I feel in despair
At your so obvious surprise
And the disappointment
Reflected in your eyes

Just once when they tell me
How lucky I was not to die
I wish I had the courage
To openly ask them why.
So, don't call me a Hero.
All I did was survive,
And I'm not quite so sure
You can call this being alive.

Love Poem For A Rainy Day

This is a love poem for a rainy day
Seem through the streaks
Of a wet windowpane
And the eyeful of streaming tears
Escaping to roll down a pale face
To be lost, absorbed with the rain.

A love poem to be read
Under open skies on
A cold wet winter morning ,
Taking comfort from walking a dog,
Faithful, nonjudgmental, offering
A wet nosed kiss,
Unconditional love and loyalty.

A love poem of sadness
For what has been lost,
Hope for what may be to come,
And a ceremonial cleansing
By cold wet pouring rain,
Washing away remnants of
A cherished past,
Regrets for what might have been,
Making clean starts
For hoped for new beginnings

Respect

She had diamonds in her eyes
I saw them flash
As she argued with her partner
A personality clash
And her gaze of ice
Just cut him down
And he grovelled.
Just like a clown
Until she smiled
And said okay
And the diamonds in her eyes
Were sheathed artfully away
Not a lady
With which to play
Then cut and run
Or slip quietly away
She had diamonds in her eyes
And a body any man would lust
But the diamonds in her eyes
Command respect and a wary trust

Learning From History

In the mid twentieth century
We copied copious notes
To be regurgitated in exams
After being learned by rote.
Just a recording of hard facts,
No speculation on the mystery
Or motivation of the incidents
In our studied period of History.
Children of the workers
For the most part
Carefully selected
To be given a start
To provide factotums that allowed
The commerce and the State,
In a class ridden capitalist system,
To efficiently and cheaply operate.

And thus for many years
We had the accepted situation
Of a compliant, controlled,
And mainly subservient nation.
Came the information Revolution
Which so very quickly seeded
The rapidly expanding situation
Where greater learning was needed.

The Universities were there
For the ambitious to get
The knowledge required but
At great accumulated debt.
Ostensibly we progressed,
The graduate class thrived,
Carefully conditioned to ensure
Capitalism so easily survived.
Since the mid twentieth century

Studies have shown
Far from reducing, the wealth gap
Has expanded and grown.
In my old age I've time to ponder
On that fascinating mystery
Why the lower orders never
Learn from the lessons of History.

Sleep

There's a peculiar type of clarity
After six hours drinking in a bar
You can maybe walk on water
Or reach out and stroke a star

The answer to so many questions
Is there clearly in your head
Tomorrow you'll tell the world
But just now you need your bed

And by the coming morning
You'll almost certainly find
Those significant thoughts will
Have been wiped from the mind

Such a tragic situation
Enough to make one weep
So many alcohol inspired insights
Just lost for the need of sleep

There's a peculiar type of clarity
After six hours drinking in a bar
You can maybe walk on water
Or reach out and stroke a star

Contingency Planning

Seven years they tracked it
Each day and night long,
The distant space mission
That very sadly went wrong.
It wasn't that the operator
Had gone and forgotten,
Just he'd sadly eaten
Something a little bit rotten.

So he'd needed the loo
In a bit of a rush
And it was ages before
He dare stand up and flush.
The time to press the button
To switch the cameras on,
A crucial few seconds, had
Very sadly passed and gone.

That's why the first photos
Of that distant alien moon
Were quickly created in
A laboratory sterile room,
And why the surface looks
Smooth flat and uncrusted
As though it was covered in
Seas of smooth yellow custard

They had to have a meeting
And that was when
It was decided they would
Need to visit that moon again.
The button pushing desk was
In future to be staffed by two
Just in case ,on the day,
One had to rush off to the lo.

And any food consumed
Has very carefully been.
Under controlled conditions
Cooked in the staff canteen.
For scientists are only human
And after all is said and done
One really can't help it if one
Has a sudden case of the runs..

The satellite is still out there
Adding to its tale of glory
Snapping new bits of space,
And enhancing a success story.
It's successor is now following
And the button man has a mate
So this time there's little chance
The camera'll be switched on late.

Music Revolutionaries

As a child of the late1940s,
Heard Skiffle, Folk, Rock and Roll
Loved country and the blues
Loved the sound of soul.
Heard, Donegan, Perkins, Presley,
Make all those blues based hits
Heard Jerry Lee, Buddy, the Bopper
Guthrie, all those talented young Brits.
Suddenly we had a language,
A music of our very own,
Criss crossing the Atlantic
To mix with that home grown.
So many decades later,
My life having moved on,
I still listen to that music but
Most of the heroes are gone

Eyes closed, glass in hand
I listen at my leisure,
My music may be old but
It gives so much pleasure.
In my mind i see my idols
Strut and own their stage
Many died too young
That just means they don't age.
Those very special people
Whose talent will not fade,
I have been so privileged to see
Music history being made.
A musical dinosaur maybe
But I don't really care.
I heard the music change
And I was lucky to be there.

red biddy ramblings

he sits there in his mansion
and he lives a life of ease
surrounded by retainers
just there to serve and please
he believes in queen and country
of that he is so sure
and he never lifts a finger
except for a manicure
he takes his seat in the lords
and regularly swaps his wife
he's a pillar of society
and leads a blameless life
but he's never danced a tango
on a deserted summer beach
drunk hoochie cheap wine
tasting like acid mixed with bleach
and he's never ever stood naked
after love over all too soon
admiring her sleeping body
beneath a great harvest moon
and he's never known that hunger
that comes from having to choose
of how to spend your last quid
on the oblivion of cheap booze
instead of the junkie food
the processed trash
that's all i can afford to buy
with my meagre amount cash
and he and his ilk
sit there and pontificate for years
on the sad ignorance
and decline of me and my peers
and he pays his advisors richly
to help him evade his tax
while he preaches of standards

he perceives as being lax
he's an officer and a gentleman
and he'll use wisely use his breath
to win that important battle
at the cost of another being's death
and when any war is over
you can bet he'll be found
picking over the spoils
from the devastation all around
he's a conservative or socialist
he doesn't really care
he just joins any party
for the profits that are there
he's a pillar of society
superb example of his kind
happy in the sanctuary of his
privileged and selfish mind

Sandman

He walks on clouds through endless night
Ever keeping one step ahead of the daylight
Endlessly circling the world of sleep
Trawling and dredging subconscious deep
Sandman never ever heard or seen
Broadcasting always the stuff of dreams
Here nice thoughts to ease a troubled mind
There harsh nightmare for one found unkind
A lover sighs a lover's contented breath
A dying dreams his way to seamless death
Some dreamers laugh some dreamers even cry
As his measured walk carries him steadily by
Sandman in his peculiar way
Eases our paths to coming day
His considerate care knows no bounds
As he walks on clouds in his endless round

jingles

you could hear the little jingle
from the assorted silver charms
hanging from the heavy bracelets
that she wore loosely on her arms

a pleasant little noise keeping
to the rhythm of making love
as I looked into her frozen eyes
wide open hovering there above
then the little jingles quickened
as emotions ran across her face
and together we both screamed
our pleasure into empty space

and the little jingles slowed
from the little silver charms
that she wore in profusion
hanging loosely from both arms

Everlasting Life

Did God invent man
For a Challenge
Or manCreate God
For an answer
We are created and recycled,
Travellers in time and space,
The latest accretion of stardust
Gathered across billions of miles
And the countless passed years
Since the Big Bang of Creation,
The Mysterious Spark.
We will drift and travel and, maybe,
In the tomorrows of eternity,
Become part of the creation of
A new born star in a fledgling galaxy.
Nothing is destroyed or lost so that,
In some form, we continue to exist,
Maybe even by chance become
Across the eons, a new sentient form
As the process cycles and recycles
Until the end, or maybe the start
Of an unimaginable new beginning.
The quest for knowledge and
Lack of answers as we strive
To know the unknowable
Is both awe inspiring and thrilling.
Will our species meet
That knowledge Wall
beyond which there is no knowing,
Or will we have long returned
Back to drifting Stardust,
Just a minor, brief incident,
In a Cosmic progression.

Self Destruction

It was a world of two ideologies
Both wanting to hold sway
Neither of which were prepared
To give anything away
Now it's a world of two Empires
Neither of which are ready to stop
But the strange thing is the same
Type of people are still at the top
The world is still full of poverty
Disease, famine and despair
But the Megalomaniacs in charge
As always just don't care.
Nobody seems to find
The situation rather odd
The destruction each will cause
In pursuit of their form of god
And very few seem prepared
To ask the question why
That pursuit pf power requires
Many millions may have to die
Perhaps it's nature's way of stating
In a form both graphic and succinct
It's very nearly the time for
Mankind to go extinct.

Black And White Days

It's like looking back through
A monochromed dream
To those long past days of
A little blood in my alcohol stream
And every day started
Like the one just passed
Only the calendar confirming
It was not the last.
The pounding thumping
Throbbing head
As I struggled from
My clinging bed
Most days
Giving thanks
That the night gone wasn't
Again a complete blank
Praying for the strength
To just carry on
Until the hangover
Was finally gone
And the time for that next beer
Was finally gratefully here.
I marvel that I am still alive
That I got the strength to survive

Natural Selection

Welcome to My Shopping Plaza
Reserved purely for the best,
Entry initially is only by passing
Our Received Pronunciation Test,
Closely followed by meeting
Our test of personal wealth.
(No well spoken impoverished
Slipping in by stealth.)
When it comes to shortlisting
I'm afraid you'll be needing
More than adequate proof of
Good blood and good breeding.

Be assured everything we sell
Is the epitome of nice
You've evaded our selection if
You have to ask the price.
We've taken every precaution to
Ensure the elite can enjoy
An afternoon of leisured shopping
Away from the common Hoi Poloi.
We d no bias again the lower orders
Most of them behave quite well
And, to be strictly honest only
A minority of them actually smell.

The working class in fact do have
Their place and their use
Even if they do at times require
Protection from our abuse.
Oh, God's still in his Heaven and
His work is more than complete
When affording privilege and style
To that deserving wealthy elite.
There's nothing wrong with equality

In fact I'll give it a toast
So long as they accept that some
Are more equal than the most.

Once your membership is accepted
All our facilities are free
On receipt of course, of our modest
Annual renewal Fee.
We do ask members to accept
That if they bring a guest
They too are expected to pass
Our modest membership test
Welcome to my Shopping Plaza
Safe in the knowledge that's it's true
It's designed for the convenience of
That deserving minority just like you.

Old Friend ii

I sit there quietly reading
As you sleep in your chair.
Sometimes I wonder if
You even know I'm there.
We used to talk and laugh
Some reminiscing talks
Youthful adventures on
Our long country walks.

Talk about chatting girls,
You always had success
I nervous and tongue tied
Didn't do that verbal chess
The weekly Hornsea dance
Admiring your pulling power
As I stood there lonely,
The classic wallflower.

We progressed through life
In our different ways
But always stayed linked
By shared teenage days.
The birthday phone calls
That never seemed to end
So many miles away but
Still my old best friend.

The unanswered phone calls
Told me something was wrong
Then I traced you to here
It didn't really take too long.
Slowly you stopped talking
Had trouble staying awake
I don't want you to be alone
I'm here for friendships sake

So I sit thinking and reading
Watching you slowly fade,
Thinking of our lives
The decisions we both made.
I am watching you progress to
An apparently peaceful end
Dreading that day when
I say goodbye to my old friend.

On Continuous Creation

And, so there was an emptiness,
Barren, sterile devoid.
Imagine the unimaginable
An endless dark dark void.
An act of instantaneous creation
That rippled on and on
So before it got where it was going
The beginning had gone,
Moving ever onward, spreading
A vast and nebulous glob
Speeding on ever faster
A constantly expanding probe.
At its centre a near emptiness
In an act of thinning
As the expanding outer edges
Were pursued by their beginning..
Chaos creation and destruction
Galaxies stars born and dying
Expanding infinities
Gravity defying.
At the epicentre
Will there come a time when
In that expanding emptiness
The process will start again,
Dimensions and parallels
In a never ending race
To briefly occupy a position
In the growing vastness of space.
Is there a place for a deity
In this suggested creation scheme
Or is it just a construct, a result
Of mankind's egoistical dream,
To explain the inexplicable.

Human Relations

The boss is in his office
and boy isn't he mean,
a short fat big gutted
misery making machine.
I reckon he's got problems
at home with his wife
the way every morning
he messes with my life.
He's supposed to raise moral
but the way her stomps around
he's driven any good spirits
way down into the ground.
You can see all the guys
with barely concealed hate
wincing with relief as he picks
his daily victim to humiliate.
He's a little tyrant and oh lord
just to have him there
for a refreshing five minutes
working on a drill square.
But the recession is on,
little chance of another job
so we all stand and squirm
while he shoots off his gob.
Just last month we all got
a company mobile phone
so even out of the depot
he won't leave us alone.
I'm stood there imagining
the pain in his eyes
if I went and drove my knee
right up between his thighs.
At last he's stopped ranting;
we're only twenty minutes late
as we walk to the vans

and drive out of the gate.
In just twenty four hours
we'll be back here and then
the whole miserable process
will start up again.
We'll all stand there
wanting to be away
each one thinking please
don't pick on me today.

White Rum and Coke,

A White Rum and Coke,
Two cubes of ice,
Tastefully decorated with
A fresh lemon slice.
First of the night
Lifted to the lips,
Appreciate the aroma,
Take a first little sip,
Then down the rest
Taken all in one,
Warmth in the stomach
The last hangover gone.
For all the rest
Dispense with the ice
Just the rum and coke,
No decorative slice.
The night starts swimming
In a sea of chat and faces.
The world is your oyster,
These your favoured places,
The world and his mate
Become your instant friend
Lovingly cherished until
That long night's end.
Awake in the morning
In a half empty bed,
Start off the day with
Thudding throbbing head.
Work through the shift
Trying not to think
Of the coming evening
And that day's first drink.
Just for a while
Not a single care
The alcohol killing

All sadness and despair
A White Rum and Coke
Two cubes of ice
Tastefully decorated with
A fresh lemon slice.

Trauma

Part 1
Leaders in splendid isolatrion
Barely seem to pause for breath
Before they sign those orders
Committing thousands unto death.

For nearly twenty years
They occupied Afghanistan
In an effort to defeat
An obdurate Taliban,
Then suddenly decided,
When the going got tough
It was time to retreat,
That enouth was enough.
Very little thought for
Lives and hopes destroyed
When they withdrew
All those forces deployed.
A country in ruins
A people in despair
Economic sanctions adding
To the chaos left there..
For nearly twenty years
They occupied Afghansitan
Before they handed it back
To a jubilant Taliban

Trauma
Part 2

When they left Afghanistan
With seeming undue haste
How many veterans thought
Their effort had been to waste
How many Pretty Pollys
Couldn't stand life's stress
Committing suicide rather than
Endure Traumatic Distress.
How many Johnnys
Now sit in despair
Restricted to the confines
Of an electric wheelchair
For nearly twenty years
They occupied Afghansitan
Seemingly handing it back
With little thought or plan.
When you occupy a country
It isn't good enough
Just to withdraw
When the going gets tough.

Leaders in splendid isolatrion
Barely seem to pause for breath
Before they sign those orders
Committing thousands unto death.

Street Walker

She was only a whore they said
Just a druggie on the game
Most of the papers couldn't be
Bothered to correctly spell her name.
Just an illegal immigrant tart,
Part of one of those foreign mobs
Over here to claim our benefits
Ot take over all of our jobs.
Not one of your high class call girls
Who service the Commons and Lords
Free of the general approbation
Such elevated status affords.

Not your enthusiastic amateur
Who put it about for free
Or one of those who've made it
By appearing on reality TV.
Not your free loving aristocrat
Hopping gaily from bed to bed
No, just a common street walker
Who unfortunately ended up dead.
Having so dehumanised her as
Just another lump of dead meat
Who earned herself a living by
Selling cheap sex on the street

This allegedly Christian nation
Doesn't really bother anymore,
Just turns to the sports page
For the latest footie score,
Or, the very wealthy
With no real material cares,
To financial pages to check
Returns on stocks and shares.
Some mother, father or child

Who won't see her anymore
Are suffused with pain and grief
Even though she was just a whore.

Wealth

A farm labourers cottage
Just two up, two down,
Streets, roads lanes, twisty
Country miles from any town.
Black leaded Yorkist Range
For the cooking and the heat,
Scrubbed farmhouse table
Where we'd all sit and eat.
Brick copper in the kitchen
Steaming proudly away,
Dolly tub, dolly stick, posher
Every weekly wash day.
Just yards from the Church
And the old burial ground
Encircled by the trees as if
Guarding each grave's mound.

Each morning I would listen,
To their whisper rustle and creak
Seeming never ever to be still,
A solemn but chatty little clique.
A constant background murmur
That seemed to flow and spread
To include me in their gossip
Warm and snug in my bed.
An almost mystical experience
To start each single day
A sort of enchanted stillness
As the trees chatted away.
There was always birdsong
Which I suppose would please
But for me the joy was to listen
To those singing, talking trees.

Just a farm labourer's cottage,

Town twisty country miles away,
Considered barely adequate
By the standards of today,
But, wealth isn't just possession
Not everybody got the pleasure
Of lying listening to my trees
Moments I'll always treasure.

Slipping Away.

I came into this world quietly,
I hope to leave in the same way
But I shall rail against injustice
My every single surviving day.
I appreciate my actions may upset
That rather large growing band
That thinks thing don't happen if
They stick their heads in the sand.
There may be poor and sick
Who are finding life so hard
But it really doesn't exist
If it's not in their back yard.
There may be a leadership
Of the affluent and the elite
Who find no contradiction in
That they steal, lie and cheat.
They can go worship on Sunday
If it's forgiveness they seek,
That keeps them shriven until
The same time next week.
Me , I'll keep on campaigning
Until my very end
Accept I see things differently
From some of my friends.
Just wish me luck and success
Fighting for what I see as right
Until peacefully and quietly I
Hopefully slip away in the night.

The Fish Stealer

She sits on the County Council now
A Person of some local status
But to me she's just person who
Went and stole my fish

It was closing time at the pub
About half past eleven I think
And as the duty driver I'd not
Had any alcohol to drink.
So it was off to the chippy
For our Friday night treat
Fried fish and taties
To take home and eat.
Fish and chips four times I ordered
One each for them and one for me.
When it came to the chips that was fine
But for the fish she only packed three.

I asked her politely to check
As one of our fish was missing.
Angrily she reacted like a kettle
Spitting and boiling and hissing
She been working here for years
She said who was I did I think
To come and make accusations
When I was full of drink
My friends though i was mistaken
And I said that's just fine
But when we sit down to eat
The one that's missing isn't mine.

Of course we unpacked
As soon as we got there
And being all close friends
We agreed for once to share

For one of our fish was missing
That server from down south
Hadn't engaged her brain
Before she'd opened her mouth .
Now i'm a Yorkie born and bred
And my memory is just fine
And I never ever forget one
Who's been rude to me and mine

She's still a County Councillor
Still a person of local status
But to me she's just thar gobby bird
Who went and stole my fish.

For Services Rendered

There were rumours running rife
About some smug smiling faces
Who ruled the Hoi Poloi
From that highest of places.

She was the Queen of gentle bondage.
Couldn't or wouldn't hurt a fly,
Practised her art with tenderness
Which was maybe the reason why
She worked the Corridors of Power
In the Houses of Commons and Lords
With her chains of gentle linen,
Soft plastic knives and swords
Handcuffs of lace and latex,
Whips of finest spider silk,
Synthetic leather face masks
As caressing as warm milk.
So all those noble worthies
Who from birth had been used
To punishment from their nannies
And Public School peer abuse
Could carry on their fettishes
Without any fear or shame
Knowing the Queen of Gentle bondage
Would never ever disclose a name
They could attend committees and
Divisions free of any mark or bruise
Which if the Red Tops had discovered
They would have broadcast on the news.
With her own chamber in the House,
An appointment book ram full
For this gentle entrepreneur
Working life was never dull.
So she practised her profession
Without any malice or hate

And in time she was ennobled
For Services to the State.

Those rumours still continued
But nothing was exposed
For during Parliamentary session
That lady seldom if ever closed.

Modern Day Warrior

He's a modern day warrior,
Drives his War Machine
By internet and Satnav
From his computer screen.
He can scan the world
From the sky and near space
With instruments so sensitive
It can pick out a single face.
It has given him the power,
Given him the skill
To, without warning, carry out
Any long range kill.
He's a modern day warrior
Who can, with ease and care,
Selectively destroy and murder
From his comfy Office chair.
It's the same the whole world over.
Every faction thinks they're right.
And they're prepared to defend it
By use of force and might.
Millions of years of Evolving
To bring mankind to this state
Of preaching love and peace
And practising murder and hate.

Other works by this author are available as paperbacks and ebooks from Amazon.

www.poetrypoem.com/smallsteps

email: madpote@yahoo.com

All poems in this book are subject to © Terry Ireland 2022

ALL RIGHTS RESERVED

This book contains material protected under Copyright Laws. Any unauthorised reprint or use of this material is prohibited. No part of this book may be reproduced or transmitted in any form or by any means, including photocopying, recording or by any information storage and retrieval system without express written permission from the author